BISHOP JAMES GRIFFIN

THEY WERE THERE

WITNESSES TO THE **PASSION OF JESUS**

TWENTY-THIRD PUBLICATIONS

 185 WILLOW STREET • PO BOX 180 • MYSTIC, CT 06355
TEL: 1-800-321-0411 • FAX: 1-800-572-0788
E-MAIL: ttpubs@aol.com • www.twentythirdpublications.com

The Scripture passages contained herein are from the *New Revised Standard Version of the Bible*, copyright © 1989, by the Division of Christian Education of the National Council of Churches in the U.S.A. All rights reserved.

Twenty-Third Publications
A Division of Bayard
185 Willow Street
P.O. Box 180
Mystic, CT 06355
(860) 536-2611 or (800) 321-0411
www.twentythirdpublications.com
ISBN:1-58595-312-1

Library of Congress Catalog Card Number: 2003113261
Printed in the U.S.A.

Contents

Introduction

The story of the final hours of Jesus' life is one we all know well—perhaps too well. We have heard this story so often, we are so familiar with the details, we have relived this story so many times in the liturgies of Holy Week, that we can easily miss its full impact on our lives. To benefit from the repetition of this most familiar story, perhaps we have to look at the story in a different light or from a new viewpoint.

During this Lent, let's prepare for those precious last days of Jesus' life by looking at the story of his passion and crucifixion from a new perspective. Let's focus on the characters, the people involved in this story. By looking closely at each of them and his or her role in the life of Jesus, we can come to a fresh, deeper, and more effective appreciation of the story of Jesus' passion and death.

As we reflect on the role of each of these individuals, we can try and identify the strength or weakness of character in each. We can then look at our own strengths or weaknesses, and see how their experience can apply to us. And as we put together these individual, in-depth pictures of the people of the passion story, we can come to a new appreciation of the entire story. We can help ourselves look at this so-familiar story in a new light. We can lead ourselves to a fuller appreciation of Jesus' great action of love on our behalf.

If we can accomplish this goal, we will have had a very profitable lenten season.

Lord, let me approach this Lent with a new resolve and a new vision. Help me to appreciate fully the importance of this penitential season in my life and its relevance to my everyday activities. Help me also to look at the story of your passion and death with a new eye, looking past the familiar to find the message for me and for my life today.

The Disciple Who Fled

We start with the story of the young man described in Mark's gospel story of the arrest of Jesus:

> A certain young man was following him, wearing nothing but a linen cloth. They caught hold of him, but he left the linen cloth and ran off naked (Mk 14:51).

Many Scripture scholars believe that this young man was Mark himself because the story is one only found in the gospel of Mark. Only he seems to know of this incident. Hence the conclusion: Mark himself was the young man! Undoubtedly this young man, whoever he was, was a man of faith. He wanted to follow Jesus. He wanted to be there. He was bold enough to follow closely. But, when the moment of crisis came, his courage failed him, and he fled.

Isn't that the story of following Jesus for many of us? We believe, we want to follow, we want to be there, but in the moment of crisis, our courage fails us and we abandon Jesus. We flee, not from a lack of faith but because of a lack of courage or resolve.

Isn't that, for many of us, the story of the lenten season? We believe; we want to follow the lenten course with the Church; we want to be there with a program of penance, prayer, and sacrifice. We start out with an ambitious lenten program and with high hopes. But somewhere along the forty days our courage fails us, and we run away from our lenten resolve.

The good news is that, like the youth in Mark's gospel, we can always return. We can always start again. In our "running away" we can console ourselves with the realization that it is better to have tried and failed than not to have tried at all.

The secret to remaining firm in our following of Jesus in times of crisis is love. If we can keep before us the remembrance of Jesus' love for us and our love for him, we will not fail him, even in the moments of greatest crisis in our lives.

From our efforts to follow Jesus, from our efforts to live Lent with the Church, even when they end in disappointment and failure, we can slowly but surely begin to uncover the secret of success.

Lord, give me the great gift of courage. Let me quietly but firmly adhere to you in every situation in which I find myself. Give me that long vision in every situation and decision that enables me to act and react always with my love for you and the ultimate goal of my life in mind.

2

James and John

James and John, brothers and fellow fishermen, were really blessed and favored by Jesus from the moment of his call to them to become fishers of men (Mt 4:21). They were chosen from their fellow disciples to be apostles (Mt 10:2). Their special treatment continued. With Peter, they were privileged to be present at the cure of the daughter of the synagogue official (Mk 5:37) and at the transfiguration, when they glimpsed the glory of Jesus (Mt 17:1). They were present with Peter and Andrew when Jesus predicted the destruction of the temple and the days of tribulation which were to come before the end of time (Mk 13:3).

Again with Peter, they were the disciples close to Jesus as he prayed in the Garden of Gethsemane on the eve of his passion (Mk 14:33).

Their title, "Sons of Thunder," probably arose from an incident in which a Samaritan village refused to receive Jesus as he passed along the road, and the brothers asked the Lord if he wanted them to call down fire from heaven to destroy the town. This received only a rebuke from Jesus (Lk 9:54).

Privileged but not yet satisfied, and not yet understanding the role of service to which they were called, the two came to Jesus (Mk 10:35–45) and asked him to give them "whatever we ask of you." When asked to be specific, they requested to sit at Jesus' right and left hand in his glory. Jesus' response and the indignation of the other apostles introduce a beautiful teaching by Jesus on the service to which his followers are called.

James and John seemed to have learned this lesson well, as Paul, when writing to the Galatians, refers to the brothers as pillars of the Christian community along with Peter (Gal 2:9).

Blessed as we are in our own discipleship, we can fall into the same mindset, seeing discipleship as a position of honor and privilege rather than as a call to service in the community. The reality is the greater our blessings, the clearer our call to discipleship, the greater is our responsibility to serve others.

Father, help me to learn that the road to greatness as a disciple is the road of service, that first place among your disciples goes to one who is the servant of all.

The Roman Soldiers

When I was a young boy attending Stations of the Cross in my parish church, I envisioned the Roman soldiers as the real villains of the passion story. Now, as an adult, I have a different and a bit softer interpretation of their role.

While not absolving them for their actions, I realize that these soldiers were products of their pagan culture. They were trained to do their job, and that is what they were doing. They had no Christian moral law to live by. They had no regard for those who were not Roman citizens. Their actions in this drama showed them to be hardened and coarse men. They were products of their times.

But what about us? We are the products of a Christian culture; we have Christian morals and ethics. We come from a culture which, at least on the surface, extends equal regard to each and every human being.

But are there parts of our lives, especially our professional or work lives, in which we are content simply to do our job, to abstract ourselves from any human consideration or any human touch in dealing with others, especially those whom we judge to be in some way beneath ourselves?

Are there situations in our lives where we neither extend nor accept any personal touch or human consideration, simply because it makes life easier for us? Perhaps there are even situations where we enjoy making a fool of others, merely because it makes us look good or gives us the impression of having power over others.

For you and for me, unlike the Roman soldiers, doing our job always includes care and concern for the person of others. We can't just do our job, whatever that job is, without including the human touch, if we are to be faithful to our baptism and to our Catholic heritage.

Lord, help me to preserve the human touch in every situation of life. Instead of looking for the easy disposition of problems or people, for the convenient way out, for the easiest response for me, grace me with the ability to look past the obvious and see the person with whom I am dealing. And let me see you in that other.

4

The Crowd in the Garden

Drawing from what we read in the Scriptures and from our own experience, we can construct a pretty good picture of the crowd that came out to the garden with those who were coming to arrest Jesus. Some were leaders sent by the chief priest and the elders, with a very definite purpose and goal, to take Jesus. Some were friends of Judas, led by him. Some were carrying clubs and swords, looking for or expecting trouble. Some were merely curious—"inquiring minds want to know." Some were just swept along by the group.

By their very presence, whatever the motivation which brought them to the garden, each member of this crowd gave authenticity to those who came out to arrest Jesus. Their presence in the crowd also undoubtedly emboldened the leaders of the crowd to carry out the action they contemplated.

Sometimes when we go with the flow of a crowd, the result is positive. But more often than not, when we allow ourselves to be swept along by the crowd we end up in situations and places we never would be in if we had followed our own inclinations. Following the crowd, allowing ourselves to be swept along by the inclination or intentions of others, or merely going along with the crowd out of idle curiosity, or because this course of action is easier, is the downfall of many. The crowd can deal a deadly blow to our fragile discipleship.

Reflection on the makeup of this crowd which came out to arrest Jesus should cause each of us to reexamine those areas of life where we simply allow ourselves to be swept along by the crowd, letting others determine our course of action, our choices, our moral positions.

Resisting the pull of the crowd is always difficult. But doing so allows us to be our own person and to choose the positions and the situations we wish to be in.

Father, give me the strength and insight to consider carefully the "crowds" I meet in moral, social and professional life. Direct my personal choices along the path you have marked out for me, not just the easy, popular, or convenient paths.

5

Malchus

Malchus, the servant of the high priest who had his ear cut off during the arrest of Jesus, is mentioned in all four of the gospels, but his treatment is different in each of them.

Mark reports only the essential elements: one of those standing nearby drew a sword, struck the servant of the high priest, and cut off his ear. Only John identifies the servant by name, Malchus, and also names Peter as the wielder of the sword. Only Luke, identified by tradition as a physician, records the cure of Malchus, reporting that Jesus touched his ear and he was cured. And only in Matthew's account, does Jesus warn his disciples following the incident with Malchus: "Put your sword back into its place; for all who take the sword will perish by the sword" (Mt 26:52).

In that warning lies a lesson for all of us. Our natural instinct is to pay back evil with evil, to meet force with force. Through his encounter with Malchus, Jesus models for us the ideal Christian response to the forces of violence and evil. He teaches us, by word and action, to refrain from the instinctive human response. More, Jesus seeks to repair as best he can the damage done by Peter's impulsive gesture, and in so doing he extends forgiveness to Malchus.

How desperately our world needs this lesson of the inability of force and violence to bring about anything but increased force and more violence. This lesson is true on the personal level, in interpersonal relationships, in the home and family, in our national society, and in international relations. In all of these venues, force has been tried over and over again and always succeeds only in generating increased force and violence. Responses laced with anger and violence only serve to feed and promote the cycle of violence.

While the natural inclination is to meet force with force and to respond to violence with violence, the Christian response demands a nonviolent stance, except in the most extreme of situations.

By word and by example, Jesus uses the presence of Malchus and his injury to teach us this great lesson. To overcome force and violence, we have to turn to the more powerful weapons of peace and forgiveness. As disciples of Jesus, men and women baptized into his redeeming death and his life-giving resurrection, we are called to be people of peace and forgiveness in every circumstance and every situation of life.

Father, make me an instrument of your peace. Help me in my daily life to resist the natural reaction to violence. Rather, let the Christian principles of peace and forgiveness permeate my response to violence on every level and in every situation of life.

6

Judas

Judas, as we all know, was the man who betrayed Jesus for thirty pieces of silver. Then he regretted his action, threw the money down in the temple, and went out and hanged himself (Lk 22:48, Mt 27:3–10).

We could reflect on the times that we have betrayed Jesus, often for much less than a bag full of silver. Even more profitably, we could reflect on the unbelievable forgiveness which Jesus offers to us always and in every circumstance.

Judas had half of the formula of repentance and forgiveness: he saw the enormity of his own sins. This is a great grace, a grace many in our present-day society often seem to miss. But the second half of the formula is equally if not more important: to recognize the extent of the forgiveness which Jesus offers us.

It is in the passion story, the *Catechism of the Catholic Church* tells us,

> that sin most clearly manifests its violence and its many forms:
> unbelief, murderous hatred, shunning and mockery by the lead-

ers and the people, Pilate's cowardice and the cruelty of the soldiers, Judas' betrayal—so bitter to Jesus, Peter's denial and the disciples' flight. However, at the very hour of darkness, the hour of the prince of this world, the sacrifice of Christ secretly becomes the source from which the forgiveness of our sins will pour forth inexhaustibly. (No. 1851)

The sacrament of reconciliation is the chief means for obtaining that forgiveness. Reception of this sacrament should be part of the lenten journey for each of us. The unbounded love which God has for us takes root in us anew each time we receive this sacrament. Regular use of the sacrament helps us keep both halves of the formula in proper perspective. We see more and more clearly both the enormity of sin and the overwhelming extent of the forgiveness which Jesus offers.

Father, help me to recognize the gravity of sin during this lenten journey. Let me see how it weakens and severs our friendship. Even more, help me to appreciate your unbounded love and forgiveness, available through the sacrament of reconciliation. Move me to avail myself of this grace during this lenten journey.

7

The Accusers of Peter

All four gospels record the story of the accusers of Peter—servant girls, men standing around a warming fire, bystanders, a relative of the man whose ear Peter had severed in the garden. All these people were quick to point a finger, charging, "You, too, were one of his disciples."

We can only speculate from what we know of these accusers as to what their motives might have been. The one certainty we have is that all of them pointed the accusing finger at Peter.

The accusing finger! How familiar all of us are with it. If we review our own lives we will see the times we have pointed that finger at others, sometimes justly, sometimes very unjustly; sometimes with a good reason, sometimes from only the basest of motives.

The story of these accusers of Peter also reminds us that, sadly, many people in our world still have a penchant for pointing out the flaws and failures of others, often while ignoring their own conduct. Many still seek justification for actions which they know are wrong with the excuse, "At least I'm not as bad as _____" (you fill in the blank).

Except where we have an obligation to others or a sincere hope of helping, we should reflect long and hard before pointing a finger.

Father, sometimes I see and recognize the faults, failings, omissions, and sins of others. May those moments become opportunities for self-reflection and self-examination. May I speak out only when compelled by justice or charity.

8

Peter

We can relate to Peter and his role in the story of Jesus' passion and death. Peter's following of Jesus in this story—and throughout the gospels—is like a roller coaster ride: tremendous highs, followed by plunges to the depths. His moments of bravery and audacious impulse are matched by moments of cowardice and confused retreat.

Peter loved Jesus. Peter believed in Jesus. Peter followed Jesus. But, like all of us, Peter was weak. His humanity kept betraying his love and his loyal discipleship.

The saving grace in this story is that Peter remained open to the forgiveness of Jesus. Even though he denied Jesus three times during the events of Holy Thursday and Good Friday, he stayed close to Jesus, open to forgiveness, which Jesus granted him with a single glance.

Peter reminds each of us that we can love, believe in, and follow Jesus, and still be weak. Our humanity betrays our love and discipleship, just as Peter's humanity betrayed his. Like Peter, we are up and down in our following of Jesus. The road is seldom level and smooth for long.

Peter reminds us that, in our weakness, we must always be ready for falls, not surprised by them. And we must always remain open to the forgiveness of Jesus.

Peter reminds us that we can always come back. When we are estranged or separated from Jesus, it is not Jesus who has moved away from us. He is always there! Rather, it is we who have moved away. Since Jesus is always there, we can always step back to him, step back into his forgiving glance.

Peter's story prepares us to expect both ups and downs in our journey of discipleship.

Lord, help me to honestly acknowledge and face my weaknesses. May those weaknesses be not a source of frustration or shame in my life, but a reminder of my own humanity, a reminder of how much I am in need of your love, support, and forgiveness.

9

The Sanhedrin

The Sanhedrin was the highest court of the Jewish people. It had both religious and civil authority and was presided over by the high priest. At the time of Jesus, the high priest was Caiaphas (Jn 18:13). It was Caiaphas who had advised the Jews that it was better that one man die for the sake of all the people (Jn 18:14). They followed his lead. The Sanhedrin, then, was responsible for the death of Jesus. They took what looked like the easy way out. Rather than risk disturbing the Romans who controlled their nation, they were willing to sacrifice one of their own citizens.

There is an important lesson here for all of us. We all hold positions of authority and exercise authority of varying degrees of importance in this world. We are parents, supervisors, foremen, teachers, chairpersons, representatives, agents, religious and civic leaders. In that exercise of authority, we must hold in mind two lessons which the Sanhedrin failed to grasp.

First, in using our authority, we must strive to serve justice. We must listen objectively to all the facts, consider all the circumstances, reflect calmly and deliberately, and then decide on the basis of justice, that is, of giving each person his or her due.

Second, in exercising authority, we must not allow ourselves to take the easy way out and promote a peace at any price approach to the exercise of that authority.

In handling any authority which we hold, we could well turn to the popular directions of the prophet Micah:

> He has told you, O mortal, what is good; and what does the Lord require of you but to do justice, and to love kindness, and to walk humbly with your God? (Mi 6:8)

Father, give me the wisdom to use well the authority I possess in this world. Let me strive to serve truth and justice with that authority. Give me the courage not to be swayed by the easy solution at the cost of truth or justice.

10

The Pharisees

The Pharisees were the predominant religious party in Israel at the time of Christ's death.

The word "Pharisee" means "separated." The members of this religious group were marked out or separated from the rest of believers by their minute observance of the law.

The Pharisees were not the most conservative of all religious groups, as they allowed for and accepted oral tradition. The most conservative of religious parties at the time of Christ was that of the Sadducees, who accepted no tradition or teaching that was not found in the Pentateuch, the original five books of the Old Testament.

Being the predominant religious party, the Pharisees were much involved in this decision about what to do with Jesus. At the time of Christ the Pharisee party had degenerated into rigorism and casuistry, which had led to an exterior observance of all the little niceties of the law while lacking any religious spirit. It was this extreme of the Pharisees' position which Jesus criticized and attempted to correct in his public teaching and in his exchanges with the members of the Pharisee party.

The Pharisees, while fixed on detail, were not all wrong, nor was everything they did negative. The Pharisees made a valuable contribution to the Jewish religion, especially in the time following Christ's death. After the destruction of the temple in 70 AD they became the religious force that held the Jewish people together for centuries.

In religion today, we still have our "Pharisees," men and women caught up in the detail of observance of religious law to the detriment of its overall purpose. We still have men and women who practice the law of Christianity without any true religious spirit enlivening that practice.

Jesus sought to gently lead the Pharisees to a true vision of religious practice. He did not reject them or ignore them. He pointed out their failings, sometimes rather forcefully, while always inviting them to a new vision of religious practice.

In dealing today with those who are stuck on the details of religious practice, while lacking in the life-giving spirit of religion, we, like Jesus, should demonstrate generosity of thought toward these people and their positions.

Generosity of word comes easily. Generosity of action is a bit more difficult. Generosity of thought is even more challenging.

Father, help me to live beyond the letter of the law. May my religious observance be filled with the life-giving Spirit. May I extend generosity of word, action and especially of thought to those whose practice of religion does not correspond completely to my own.

Annas and Caiaphas

Annas and Caiaphas (Jn 18:13,24) represent "the establishment." They were the high priests. The high priests were the head of the priestly hierarchy. They had supreme authority over the temple, the worship in the temple, and the personnel who served there. They were looked upon as the mediators par excellence between God and his people. The people turned to them when faced with vexing questions, like what to do with Jesus.

Not wanting to deal with Jesus, the chief priests found a way to pass the problem on. In this story, they represent those in authority who weasel out of facing a problem. They were all too happy to pass the problem on to another rather than face it themselves.

How do we handle problems?

In our positions of responsibility in life, do we sometimes follow the course of action which the high priests adopted? Do we pass the problem on, rather than face it, even though we recognize that it is our problem to solve? How do we react to the responsibilities of our professions and jobs? And what about our responsibilities in our own vocations? What of our duties as husbands or wives, fathers or mothers?

It is part of our human nature to like the perks of the profession or position which we hold. We readily accept and claim as our own these positive advantages. It is also built into our human nature that we have a strong tendency to shy away from the responsibilities and burdens of that same profession or position. Our human inclinations make us all too willing to pass on the problems while clinging to the perks.

Every vocation in life brings responsibility with it. Every calling has its own duties and demands. "Duty" and "demand" sound like harsh words, yet they are an accurate description of the actions we have to perform at times in life because of who we are.

Father, grant me the courage to respond to the responsibilities of my situation in life. Help me not to search for ways to pass on problems or explain them away, but to face them and, with the wisdom of your Spirit, to address them.

12

Pontius Pilate

Next to the words of Jesus himself, in the passion narrative the words of Pilate are the best remembered and the most often quoted.

Reflecting on a collection of his words in this story, we might well dub Pilate the master of the one-liner in the gospels. Who could forget his "Behold the man," or "What is truth?" or "Shall I crucify your king?" or "What I have written I have written!"

The type of speech Pilate uses, the smart retort, is characteristic of a person who lives only on the surface of life. Unfortunately, this type of speech the smart retort is alive and well in our own society today. Just look at our TV programs, our books and magazines, even our everyday speech. While on occasion this kind of speech makes the user look good, it often hurts others or turns conversations from any depth of exchange or reflection, or even ends the communication.

We must learn to understand and appreciate the power of words. Our faith helps us in this effort. Look at the story of creation in the Book of Genesis. God said: "Let there be light and there was light." God named a thing and so it was. The creation story reminds us of the power of words and of the effect that words, God's or ours, can produce.

The power of words. Just reflect on your own life. Can you not remember times when another's words inflicted unbelievable pain, or stopped you short in your tracks, or simply devastated you? By contrast, can you not remember how the words of another were the source of comfort, compassion, or lifelong encouragement for you?

Words, then, do make a difference. We are called upon to respect others when we speak to them or about them. We are challenged to reflect not primarily on the effect that our words might have on ourself and our own image, but on the effect that those words might have on others and on their self-worth.

We must remember that we speak to and about others respectfully, not because of their power, or importance, or position, or authority, but because they share humanity with us.

Father, help me to penetrate to the depth of the meaning of words. May my speech demonstrate my grasp of this depth of appreciation. Grant me the grace to be respectful of the personhood of others in all my words. Let my voice be an echo of your Son's great commandment of love.

13

Pilate's Wife

As the result of a dream, Pilate's wife sent him the message to step away from condemning Jesus. "While he was sitting on the judgement seat, his wife sent word to him: "Have nothing to do with that innocent man for today I have suffered a great deal because of a dream about him" (Mt 27:19). Here was a woman who possessed the courage to speak out to the one whom she loved, when she felt that he was making a serious mistake.

How often do we refrain from doing or saying what we know is right, because of fear of ridicule or rejection? We do not speak out with courage even to those whom we profess to love the most in this world. Or we do not listen to or heed others because we have assumed a stance of superiority in regard to them or their opinions. We have made our decision; we then close our minds to any additional input.

The lesson is twofold. We need the courage to speak out and we need the humility to listen to others' piece of the truth.

We have to learn to speak out courageously. We must speak out, not to correct another, or embarrass another, or punish another, or for any other base motive. We speak out to share our conviction of truth with another, whom we accept as a fellow seeker of truth.

We also have to learn to listen. We listen to learn the truth. We listen to others because we are convinced that everyone is a seeker of truth, and in that seeking, everyone arrives at at least a part of that truth. Putting these pieces of truth together moves all of us toward the great truth, which is God.

Father, help me to recognize and pursue truth. May I realize that the truth I possess must be shared with others, whatever the risk. And may I acknowledge that others also possess part of the truth. In my search for truth, then, may I always be open to their contribution.

14

Barabbas

Barabbas and his release from prison is mentioned in all four of the evangelists' accounts of the trial of Jesus.

Barabbas was a criminal who was in prison for insurrection and murder. As it was the custom for the governor to release a prisoner at the festival time, Pilate put the question to the crowd: "Whom do you want me to release for you, Barabbas or Jesus?" The leaders of the people incited them to call for Barabbas to be released and for Jesus to be crucified. Barabbas was released because of Jesus. He was released instead of Jesus. He was snatched from the jaws of death by Jesus' sacrifice.

What happened to Barabbas? Did Jesus' saving act have any influence on his life? Did he reform? Did he become a different or a better person because of his encounter with Jesus? Again, there is much legend and speculation, but no one knows.

We cannot answer that question about Barabbas. But each of us can and must answer the question: "What happened to me after I was released because of Jesus?" Each of us has been snatched from the jaws of death by Jesus' sacrifice. Now we have to answer the question, "And then what happened?" We answer it by the way we live. We have to demonstrate by our lives that the saving action of Jesus has influenced and directed us, that we are better persons because of the presence of Jesus in our lives.

Lord, may I come more and more to appreciate your great act of loving sacrifice for me. Move me to rejoice in being loved so much by you. Especially in times of disappointment and despair, may I be comforted by the recollection of your limitless love for me.

15

The Temple Guard Who Struck Jesus

In the gospel of John, after Jesus was arrested, he was brought before Annas. When Jesus was questioned about his teaching, he told Annas that he taught in public, not in secret.

> Ask those who heard what I said to them; they know what I said. When he had said this, one of the police standing nearby struck Jesus on the face, saying: 'Is that how you answer the high priest?' (Jn 18:21–22)

The temple guard was being loyal to his image of how the high priest should be treated. He did not look past the surface situation, to see the person of Jesus. He simply reacted to his idea of how things should be and how people should behave in the presence of the high priest. He knew the situation and the appropriate response to it, or so he thought.

Don't we often react in a similar fashion? We think that we know situations. We have our expectations of how things should be and how people should react, and we do not move beyond them.

The story of the temple guard should bring home to us the necessity of widening the parameters of our vision, the necessity of thinking in new ways. We have to try to look beneath the surface and to see the person of others. We cannot allow ourselves to be locked or trapped inside the limits of our normal vision.

The perfect example of being open to a wider perception of situations arises in our consumer-oriented society every time we are waited upon by a clerk or salesperson or served by a waiter or waitress. In these situations, do we have our expectations and react strongly when they are not fulfilled when or as we expected? Or do we try to look beyond the immediate and regard this person as a human being with feelings and concerns and worries like ourselves?

Lord, shake me out of my routine and accustomed actions, especially those which insulate me from the person of others. Let me not be governed by my expectations of others, but open me to accept them as they are.

16

Herod

Herod was the younger son of Herod the Great, the king of Judea at the time of the birth of Jesus. The tetrarch of Galilee in Perea, Herod ruled at the nod of the Roman emperor. The Romans used this local ruler to keep the nationalistic tendencies of the people in check.

Pilate was the Roman ruler in the area, the procurator of Judea. He was a Roman citizen, and he ruled in the name of the emperor. His aim in life was to curry the favor of the emperor in the hopes of obtaining a more lucrative post.

Herod and Pilate, then, were at odds because they were both in charge, but from different perspectives.

Luke has a very special reason for including this story, a reason that is revealed in the last line of the description of the encounter between Jesus and Herod: "That same day Herod and Pilate became friends with each other; before this they had been enemies" (Lk 23:12).

Reconciliation is a theme that runs through Luke's gospel. He presents Jesus as the great reconciler, reconciling people to God and to each other. Luke sees the sequel to the story of Jesus appearing before Herod, that is, Herod's reconciliation with his former enemy Pontius Pilate, as a specific instance of the reconciling power of Jesus. Even as he enters into his own great action of suffering, Jesus continues to be the great reconciler. During his own trial, he brings about a reconciliation between these two estranged local rulers.

In our world today there is a great need for reconciliation, and Jesus remains the great reconciler. His example contains an object lesson on the limits of our own efforts at reconciliation. If Jesus could reconcile the two men who had but did not use the power to deliver him from death, what acceptable excuse can any of us offer for not attempting to reconcile with our enemies, or for not trying to reconcile others between whom enmity exists?

The true sign of the follower of Jesus is love without limits. The early pagans realized this. We are told that they marveled: "See how these Christians love one another!"

Christians are called to do more than forgive, as difficult as forgiveness might sometimes be. Christians are called to be ministers of reconciliation, to restore peace and harmony.

Father, keep me alert to the many opportunities in my life to be a reconciler in imitation of your Son. Give me the courage to be the initiator of offers of both forgiveness and reconciliation. Keep me always open to gestures of reconciliation extended to me by others.

17

Veronica

If you search the Scriptures for the story of Veronica, you will not find it! This story, commemorated in the sixth station in the Way of the Cross, comes to us from the rich tradition of the Church.

According to that tradition, Veronica was a woman standing along the Via Dolorosa (the "Way of the Cross"). She stepped forward, not expecting anything in return, to help someone in need. She offered Jesus a cloth with which to wipe his face. She came away, tradition tells us, with an image of his face imprinted on the cloth. This encounter with Jesus is the origin of her name: "vera" (true), "icon" (image).

Legend goes on to further identify Veronica. One story makes her the wife of Zacchaeus, who brought salvation to his house through his encounter with Jesus at Jericho. Another story makes her the woman who suffered from hemorrhages for twelve years and was cured by touching the hem of Jesus' garment. Whatever her origins, Veronica stepped forward in concern, and received the reward of a lasting image on the cloth she presented to Jesus and a lasting part in the passion story

We can all relate to Veronica and her story. We have all been on both sides of this equation of care and concern. There have been times in our lives when someone has gone out of his or her way to help us. There have also been occasions on which we have gone out of our way to help another.

We know the reward! We never forget those who have stepped forward to help us, not expecting anything in return. Nor do we forget the moments when we have stepped forward to help another in need. The reward is fixed in our memory.

More, we know that the good that we have done and do for others is rewarded by a lasting image in God's memory!

Lord, make me quick to respond to the needs of others. So often, as I mentally debate the question of going out of my way to help another, the moment passes. Help me to be quick to help others. And give me the gracious ability to accept help from others, seeing in that help, your response to my need.

Simon of Cyrene

The three synoptic gospel writers give us a good picture of Simon of Cyrene and of his role in the passion story. They describe him as a nonresident of the city of Jerusalem, one who had come in from the country. They also all agree that Simon was not eager to assist Jesus in the carrying of his cross; they speak of his being "seized," or "compelled," or "made" to carry the cross behind Jesus.

We can't be too hard on Simon. Since he had come into the city, he most likely had his own purposes, an agenda to accomplish during his visit, and here he is being forced to take up the cross of a condemned prisoner and to carry that cross with and for the condemned man. We must remember that, willingly or not, Simon did indeed carry the cross behind Jesus.

Each of us knows our own reaction when God steps into our well-planned lives and changes those plans. We all know from personal experience how difficult it is to adjust to sudden and unexpected turns in our plans. In some instances we never do adjust.

A change in our plans: it happens often in our lives. Still, it doesn't get easier to accept. I once heard a humorist ask: "Do you know how to get God to laugh?" The response: "Tell God your plans." In every bit of humor there is a kernel of truth.

It might have been a moment of grace in prayer when you clearly saw God's will for you, or it might have been a phone call from a friend requesting a favor. It might have been a neighbor asking only for a moment of your time. It might have been as simple as a stranger interrupting your schedule.

Simon's role in the passion story is a reminder to each of us of the need of flexibility in life. We must approach life knowing that our plans will often have to be changed to meet the demands, or the requests, or just the presence of others. We need to see that call to flexibility as God's will for us.

Father, give me the grace to be able to set my agenda aside when your will or the need of my brothers or sisters calls out to me. Rather than being resistive or annoyed by these zigs and zags of life, let me see them as opportunities to grow in flexibility.

19

Women of Jerusalem

As Jesus was led out to be crucified, a great number of people followed. Some were just curious, wanting to see what was happening. Others were vindictive, anxious to see this rebel punished. Still others were sympathetic. The women of Jerusalem described in the passion narrative fall into this last category. Luke tells us that they were beating their breasts and wailing for Jesus.

These women were standing alongside the Via Dolorosa because they felt for Jesus. It is characteristic of women to be sympathetic to the troubles of other human beings. These women stood at the side of the road and expressed their empathy with Jesus.

Having walked these same narrow streets of the Way of the Cross in Jerusalem, I can easily picture these beshawled women, pressed against the building at the side of the narrow road, crying out to and for Jesus as he passed by on the way to his crucifixion.

The presence of the women of Jerusalem in the story of the crucifixion is a reminder to all of us that we should take leave from our own daily cares and concerns and go to the side of the road of life, to be concerned about others and their sufferings. We are called to do this not so much for the sake of the other, though our expression of concern and sympathy will surely help them in the midst of their sorrow, but because to be truly and fully human and to walk authentically in the footsteps of Christ we must respond to the needs of others.

In our response to their difficulties we will find the fullness of our own humanity and of our Christian calling.

Jesus underscores this lesson for us when, in the midst of his own death march, he notices these women, turns to them and expresses his own sympathy for their coming woes. Setting aside the human tendency to turn in on self in the midst of suffering, Jesus concerns himself with the situation of these women. What a powerful picture he presents for our imitation!

In our own lives, when burdens, hardships, sufferings, discouragement and self-pity press in upon us, how natural it is to turn in on oneself. But, as we learn from experience and from the example of Jesus and the women of Jerusalem, relief is found in turning outward to others.

Father, give me the sensitivity always to be aware of others and their sufferings. And in times of my own trials grant me the grace to reach out to others, knowing that the road to the solution of my own difficulties lies through them.

20

The Thief
Crucified with Jesus

Christian tradition refers to one of the men crucified with Jesus as "the good thief." Why do we call him "good"? Because he opened himself to grace and accepted the salvation which Jesus offered. Listen to one of the great Fathers of the Church, Cyril of Jerusalem:

> After all, he saved the thief on the holy hill of Golgotha because of one hour's faith; will he not save you too, since you have believed? (*The Office of Readings*, Wednesday of the Thirty-first Week).

This man was saved because of his faith. His faith was strong enough to overcome his sins of theft and all the other offenses of a lifetime. His moment of faith should be encouragement to us who have struggled for a lifetime of faith.

Christian tradition characterizes this man as the good thief. But what is good about a thief? He is also sometimes described as the thief who stole heaven. But we know that no one steals heaven. It takes work on our part and openness to and acceptance of God's great gift of faith.

With that lesson in mind, reread the story of the good thief (Lk 23:39–42). The obvious lesson in this exchange with Jesus on the part of this man is the power of faith.

Faith, as Jesus himself told us, has the power to move mountains (Mt 17:20). To attain salvation, we have to believe.

Father, give me the gift of faith. Like the good thief, may I open myself to grace and accept the salvation which Jesus offers. Father, I do believe. Help my unbelief.

21

The Passersby
Who Taunted Jesus

The bystanders who mocked Jesus remind us of how little human nature has changed in two thousand years.

Some people are quick to jump at the juicy details or the contradictions which surround every human tragedy. Rather than centering on the humanity of the one involved in the tragedy, they dehumanize the situation. In this way they shield themselves from the natural human sentiments of empathy and understanding which arise when we witness the suffering of another human being. At the same time they enable themselves to launch their own barbed words with impunity.

It seems that once we can remove the humanity of another from the situation before us, the victim diminishes in importance and the taunter or attacker grows in importance. Witness the pro-life struggle, in which, once the humanity of the human fetus is removed, "pro-choice" arguments can seem rational and convincing.

When we have an enemy, individual or collective, we work to dehumanize that person or those people. Once we succeed in this effort, we can attack and criticize freely; empathy and understanding are effectively removed from the equation.

Unfortunately, we can never renew the humanity of another. And when we strive to dehumanize another, every degree of success removes that much of our own humanity. The bottom line is that the only one we can succeed in completely dehumanizing is self.

The opposite also stands true. The more we can reach out to the humanity of another in empathy and understanding, the stronger our own humanity becomes. Total success here results in us always seeing first, in every situation, the humanity of our sisters and brothers.

Lord, help me to grow in my appreciation of my own worth and value by reaching out in sympathy, empathy, and understanding to every sister and brother I meet on the road of life. Never allow me to degrade my own worth and value by deliberately attacking the worth and value of any other human life.

The Soldiers Who Crucified Jesus

The soldiers involved in the crucifixion are essential to the story of the passion. They are presented in a matter-of-fact fashion. After all, they were just following orders. They were just behaving in the way that soldiers in their culture were expected to behave. Their treatment of Jesus, from the seizure in the garden, through the mocking, and the crowning with thorns, to the crucifixion and the piercing of his side by a lance, were within the parameters of the expected behavior of a Roman soldier.

There are a lot of us today who accept the parameters of our culture as the limits of our own behavior. Our first questions about a proposed course of action are: "Is it legal?" "Is it politically correct?" "Is it acceptable among my peers?" If the answer to these questions is affirmative, we feel justified in moving forward in action.

Look at how often these questions or variations of them rule our business life, our family life, even our social and recreational life.

For the serious Christian the first point of reference should not be what our culture expects of us, but rather what our faith expects of us.

Our first questions should be: "Is it moral?" Then, we can ask: "What is the likely effect on the needs and sensitivities of others?"

If this is not the framework in which we weigh our actions, if what our culture expects or allows sets the parameter of our decisions, we are not too different from these Roman soldiers.

It is easy to determine which of these approaches rules our life. One or the other of these very different sets of questions—those from our culture or those from our faith—leaps to mind each time we are confronted with a choice or a decision in life. That set of questions tells us what rules our life—the expectations of our culture or the expectations of our faith.

We find that what rules our life is the truth that we accept as the solid rock basis of our person. These beliefs form our character. These beliefs mold our decisions. These beliefs, as the foundation of our lives, animate our actions.

Father, help me to be countercultural in the Christian sense of the word, that my decisions and actions be guided by the truths of faith and not the whims of society. Let my attitudes and actions give proof of my Christian faith.

23

The Bystander Who Offered Jesus Wine

It is very interesting that all four evangelists record one small act of human kindness in the final moments of the life of Jesus.

When Jesus cries out, "I am thirsty," one of the bystanders dips a sponge in a mixture of cheap wine and hyssop and raises it to the lips of Jesus to both allay his thirst and ease his pain.

This action is also the fulfillment of a prophecy in Psalm 69, where the psalmist continues to trust in God even in the midst of pain and suffering (Ps 69:21).

In the midst of this story of unbelievable pain and suffering, we have preserved forever this one simple act of human kindness.

There is a general lesson as well as a more specific lesson here for our everyday lives. The general lesson is that of human sensitivity. We have to strive to be aware of others always, to be sensitive to their needs and their cries for help in words or in actions.

More specifically, the lesson is that in the final moments of life for those whom we love or serve or live with, we have to realize how important it is to be sensitive and to reach out to them. At this time the gift of presence comes to have unbelievable value.

The simplest act of awareness, of empathy, of friendship, of love, takes on profound significance. These acts can have consequences unknown to us but of eternal significance. And those who have lost a loved one never forget the kindness and empathy of others expressed in that moment.

Father, grant me the great gift of sensitivity to my brothers and sisters. In every moment and situation of life, help me to heed their call and to reach out to them in presence and love.

24

The Women at the Foot of the Cross

Meanwhile, standing near the cross of Jesus were his mother, and his mother's sister, Mary the wife of Clophas, and Mary Magdalene. (Jn 19:25)

The tiny group of women standing at the foot of the cross were the women who had followed Jesus from Galilee. These were women filled with compassion, love, and devotion. They were loyal to Jesus; they were a courageous group. They were not shamed by others into stepping away from Jesus.

Even though all that they could do was to stand by and watch the unfolding of the crucifixion event, they were there. By their mere presence, they provided encouragement and strength to the dying Jesus. Their steadfast presence prompts reflection for us to apply to our own lives.

How often do we allow embarrassment to cause us to step away from Jesus? How often, because of the influence of others, do we compromise, cut corners, save face at the cost of our own discipleship? And we absolve ourselves with the excuse: "Well, I could not have done much anyway."

How often do we miss the significance of the virtue of presence, of just being there for others? How often do we fail to recognize what a source of encouragement and support our mere presence can be to others, especially when they are suffering or in the midst of a moral dilemma or a difficult decision?

Love and devotion cannot always be expressed in action. Love and devotion do not always demand, nor even always allow action. Like the women standing silently at the foot of the cross, we often express our love and devotion to others precisely through the great gift of presence.

Lord, help me appreciate the great gift of presence. Let me share that gift with others, being with them in their sorrows, sickness and disappointments, even when that presence is all that I can offer. And give me the gift of appreciating the presence of others to me. May their presence to me be a sign of your love for me.

25

John

John is a faithful friend. He is the disciple who stuck with Jesus to the end. He is the apostle who was not afraid to show his love for Jesus. He is the one who was given the custody of Jesus' own mother from the lips of Jesus himself (Jn 19:25–27).

Everyone appreciates a faithful friend. We recognize that quality quickly in others. We are complimented when this description is applied to ourselves. A faithful friend is characterized by communication and service: Friend communicate regularly with each other and stand ready to serve each other in any capacity possible.

Communication involves regular and significant sharing. With a true friendship, we search for frequent opportunities to enter into intimate dialogue. Standing ready to serve means again, that, we seek out, we search for ways in which we can serve the needs of our friend. Without being asked we step forward to offer our assistance. When asked, we bear any hardship or sacrifice in order to respond in a positive manner to the request of our friend.

Our friendship with Jesus is no different than our friendships with other people in this regard. That friendship also is marked by communication and service. We communicate with Jesus through prayer and the sacraments, especially the Eucharist. We serve Jesus when we serve one another (Mt 25:40). Our friendship with Jesus is our most vital friendship in life.

Father, may I always be the faithful friend of your Son, Jesus. May I stay with Jesus to the end. May I never shirk from demonstrating my love for him. May I serve him in my sisters and brothers, and may I hear from your own lips those final words of judgment: "Well done, good and faithful servant."

26

Mary

We now turn the spotlight on Mary, the mother of Jesus. Mary is the *mater dolorosa,* the sorrowful mother, the central grief figure among all of the persons connected to the suffering and death of Jesus.

Mary was and remains full of grace, "our tainted nature's solitary boast," but these privileges did not shield her from the sufferings of life, nor did they make life perfectly understandable to Mary. In point of fact, her sensitive grace-filled nature most likely made the sufferings of life even more profound for her.

Think of the suffering Mary went through trying to reconcile the joy-filled and uplifting message of the annunciation with the death-bearing and depressing message of the cross on which her son hung dying. Just think of the suffering she went through trying to understand the life of her own son.

Her senses and emotions must have cried out to her during that pitiful death of her son that something was terribly wrong here. It could not, in any conceivable way, appear that the God of the annunciation and the God of the crucifixion could be harmonized. How could the wood of the stable and the wood of the Cross possibly correspond? How could the angel of the annunciation be reconciled with the angel of death?

Mary's fullness of grace enabled her to bear these immense sorrows and these troubling questions in humble acceptance of God's will, hidden as it may be from human understanding. Her obedient acceptance enabled her to take the long view of life, to wait with confident expectation for the reconciliation beyond the parameters of human experience, a confidence rewarded three days later in the resurrection of her son from the dead.

So often in life we find ourselves in a position similar to Mary, filled, almost overwhelmed, with sorrow, with unanswerable questions on our mind, with no possible human explanation of the affliction confronting us. In these sufferings, we must turn confidently to Mary, the sorrowful mother. We have to lay our suffering humbly at her feet and ask her to intercede for us with her Son for acceptance and understanding.

Mary, mother of sorrows, help me in the midst of my suffering. Give me that obedient acceptance of the will of the Father. Obtain for me the grace to preserve the long view of life that rests in confident trust in the loving plan of God for my salvation.

27

The Centurion

The centurion was the Roman officer in charge of the soldiers who crucified Jesus. These same soldiers were most probably the ones who had seized Jesus in the garden the night before, brought him from one authority to another, scourged him, mocked him, and crowned him with thorns, herded him along the Via Dolorosa, nailed him to the cross, cast lots for his clothes, and stood watch over his final agony, even then, still making sport of this "king of the Jews." They were hard men, and their leader was a hard man.

But when Jesus died, nature itself reacted. Darkness covered the land. The veil in the temple was rent in two. There was an earthquake, rocks were split in two, graves were opened. The centurion, the man in charge of inflicting shame, suffering and death on Jesus, took in all these signs of the time. He grasped their import. He applied what he grasped to the present moment and he cried out, "Truly this man was God's Son!" (Mk 15:39)

Undoubtedly there were many in the crowd who failed to connect the darkness, the earthquake and the other signs of nature to Jesus' death. Others may have made the connection but failed to draw that connection out to its logical conclusion. Still others came even this far but then failed, out of fear or other human considerations, to voice their conclusion.

How often in life do we move easily along, failing to heed the signs of our time? How often do we note these signs but fail to make any application of their message to our own situation? How frequently do we heed and correctly interpret the meaning of the signs of the time and apply them to our own lives, but then fail out of fear or other human considerations to give voice to our conclusions? We shrink back from admitting our previous lack of understanding. We hesitate to share the truth we have discovered with others.

Recognizing the signs of the time requires quiet reflection. We must quiet ourselves in order to see the activity of God in our world and in our own lives. Responding to this awareness means that we open ourselves to the activity of the Spirit.

Father, give me the presence and power to read the signs of the times in my life. Grant me the insight to correctly interpret these signs for my own spiritual journey. Give me the strength to apply that wisdom in my life and to share what I have learned with others.

28

Longinus

Only John reports the story of the soldier who pierced Jesus' side with a spear: "…one of the soldiers pierced his side with a spear, and at once blood and water came out" (Jn 19:34).

Commentators who follow the richly, theological meaning that John puts into his stories often see a special significance in this moment of the passion. The blood and the water which flowed out from the side of Christ are for John symbols of baptism and the Eucharist.

Tradition holds that the name of this soldier was Longinus. We include this soldier in our story of the witnesses to passion for a very special reason.

As John tells us in his gospel, not everything that Jesus said or did is recorded in the Scriptures. The story of Longinus reminds us that there are many people of the passion story who are not included in the four evangelists' accounts of the final day of Jesus' life. Many of these stories have been lost many others have been handed on to us by the traditions of our Church, outside of the gospels.

In that fact lie two important lessons for us as we reflect on the suffering and the death of Jesus.

First, we have to realize and acknowledge that there are many people of the passion event who are not identified or even described in the gospels. Tradition supplies accounts of many of these individuals. We should not be quick, to dismiss as meaningless or without value the stories that we find in the traditions of our faith.

Secondly, the story of Longinus reminds us that there were a host of individuals present at the passion and death of Jesus who are not named, or even included in the story. Yet many of them are as important and significant as those who names and stories are highlighted in the evangelists' accounts.

The story of Longinus reminds us that in our own world all of us, while remaining for the most part nameless and unrecognized, are significant in the present story of God's relationship with his people, as Was Longinus in the story of the death of Jesus. Unknown, unnamed, unrecognized, our part in that unfolding story of God's dealing with His people remains important. It is important to ourselves and it may well be important to countless others.

Father, may I realize throughout my life, the importance of my story in the great unfolding of Your relationship with Your sons and daughters. May I live my life in such a way that I will accomplish the special role you have marked out for me in the great story of salvation.

29

Joseph of Arimathea

Joseph of Arimathea was the man who stepped forward to ask for the body of Jesus and who supplied the tomb in which Jesus was buried.

Joseph is named in all four gospels. From these accounts we know that he was a good and honorable man and a member of the council, one who did not agree with the decision of the council to put Jesus to death. We also know that he himself was a disciple of Jesus, but a disciple in secret because he was afraid of the Jewish authorities.

But when the chips were down, when fate put him in the position to serve Jesus by acting courageously, Joseph responded. He boldly and courageously stepped forward to ask Pilate for the body of Jesus. For that act, he will be remembered until the end of time.

Joseph is a great model for us of what the grace of God can accomplish, even in a disciple who is a bit reticent, who hangs back at times because of the fear of losing human respect. Joseph's story reassures us that God's grace is a power that transcends our human abilities and strengths, a power that literally draws us out of ourselves, beyond the safe limits most of us create for ourselves in life.

Joseph of Arimathea is also a great source of hope and confidence for us as we stumble towards the Parousia. His example assures us that when the chips are down in our own life, when we are called upon to serve Jesus by acting courageously Jesus will be at our side with the gift of his grace, enabling us to do or say what we know is right, despite what anyone else may be saying or thinking or doing.

Father, give me the quiet assurance of the help of your grace to face life with calm and sureness. Help me not to be disquieted or fearful of what the future might bring in to my life. Reassure me of the presence and power of your grace when I need it, empowering me always to be the faithful disciple.

30

Nicodemus

Nicodemus appears three times in the life of Jesus. He came once to visit Jesus in the night and talk with him about baptism and being born again in the Holy Spirit (Jn 3:1–9). He defended Jesus when Jesus was on trial before the Sanhedrin, asking that in accord with the Jewish law, no decision be made in this case until Jesus was given a hearing. (Jn 7:50, 51). And, finally, he brought spices, a mixture of myrrh and aloes, to anoint the body of Jesus when it was laid in the tomb (Jn 19:39).

Nicodemus sought the truth and found the truth. But then he seemed to be paralyzed, unable to follow the truth. Nicodemus did not really step forward until it was too late. He was governed by his fear, which happens so often to all of us. We know the feeling of the tight spot he found himself in, as we have all been there ourselves.

A lesson is here for us: we have to seek the truth. In seeking the truth, we will find it. Then we have to do the one thing which Nicodemus seemed unable to do. With God's grace, we have to follow the truth, even if that following puts us in conflict with others.

We could say that Nicodemus hung around Jesus. He stayed close, without really committing himself.

How about us? Do we hang around Jesus? Or do we give ourselves to Jesus without reserve?

Lord, give me courage to be a loyal follower, whatever my fear of the cost of discipleship. Help me to be willing to seek you at all times, not just in the light of life, but also in its darkness; to defend you always, not just in the critical public moments of life; to give you honor and glory, not with spices and myrrh, but with the good works of my life.

31

The Guards at the Tomb

The guards were at the tomb because even Jesus' enemies were aware of his promise of resurrection. The chief priests and Pharisees went to Pilate, told him of this promise, and asked for a guard lest Jesus' disciples steal his body away and tell people that Jesus had been raised from the dead. Pilate told them, "You have a guard of soldiers; go make it [the tomb] as secure as you can (Mt 27:62–66).

Once Jesus did rise from the dead, the same leaders had a dilemma facing them. They had taken every precaution to forestall rumors of Jesus rising from the dead. Yet, he had risen. Their solution: they gave a large sum of money to the guards to say, "His disciples came by night and stole him away while we were asleep " (Mt 28:13). These leaders also promised protection to the guards against any action by the governor.

The guards were opportunists. It is clear that they knew the truth of who Jesus was: "For fear of him, the guards shook and became like dead men" (Mt 28:4). Yet for money and protection they were willing to sell out the truth that they knew. For material gain, they were even willing to accuse themselves of one of the greatest of military crimes, that is, sleeping when on guard duty. They were willing to sell themselves for profit.

We might ask ourselves: What would cause us to abandon the truth which we know, to sell ourselves?

The answer should be, "Nothing." But sad experience teaches us that this is not always the case. There usually isn't much time for reflections at the moment of choice or in the midst of a dilemma. Like the guards, we have the choice plunked down before us and are told, "Choose!" And, again, as in the case of the guards, the atmosphere is usually highly charged, not an ideal time to be rethinking our principles of life.

Experience should teach us that it is good to reflect on these questions from time to time in moments of rest and calm to renew our resolve that indeed "nothing" shall separate us from the Lord. We have to be firm in these principles in advance of any choice or dilemma being presented to us. We have to sit back and reflect on the meaning and purpose of our lives, reaffirm our priorities, and decide anew that nothing will separate us from the Lord.

Father, give me the grace to realize that nothing, absolutely nothing, is worth being separated from you. Motivate me to reflect on and renew that resolve periodically as I move toward final and complete union.

32

Mary Magdalene

What balance and opposition we can find in God's plan for his people's salvation!

Balance. The beginning of the fulfillment of the drama of salvation was announced to a woman, Mary, the mother of Jesus. The completion of the same drama of salvation was announced to a woman, Mary Magdalene.

Opposition. The first Mary was "full of grace"; the second Mary had seven devils cast out of her by Jesus (Mk 16:9).

Mary Magdalene was probably from a small town on the shore of the Sea of Galilee, Magdala, a town that still is in existence today. She is listed among the women who followed Jesus and attended to his needs (Lk 8:2). She was present in a small group of women who loyally stayed at the foot of Jesus' cross until the end (Mt 27:56).

Along with another small group of women, Mary Magdalene discovered the open grave on Easter Sunday morning and heard the angel's announcement of the resurrection of Jesus (Lk 24:1–10), and she was the first person to see and speak to the risen Jesus (Mt 28:9).

Mary Magdalene is the consummate model of the repentant sinner and of the transformation which God's grace can effect. She is a source of great hope to all of us. In the midst of our recognition of our own sinfulness, hope is not lost. We see how even a person possessed by seven devils is not beyond the reach of the forgiving touch of Jesus.

In the numbing routine of everyday life, Mary Magdalene is a source of assurance to us that if we loyally follow Jesus, his grace will sustain us and he will indeed reward us as he rewarded Mary Magdalene, with the sight of himself in his risen glory.

Father, may the example and prayer of Mary Magdalene help me not to lose hope, even in the midst of my own sinfulness. Like her, may I struggle to keep close to your Son, knowing that in him I find forgiveness and fulfillment.

33

Lazarus

The night before his triumphal entry into Jerusalem, starting along the road that would carry him to the cross, Jesus dined at the home of Lazarus. The crowds came out of the city to see of Jesus, the Scriptures tell us, and to see Lazarus, whom Jesus had raised from the dead. The Scriptures also tell us that raising Lazarus from the dead caused many to believe in Jesus.

Our first reaction might well be: many? What does Jesus have to do to evoke the faith of all? He raises a man from the dead and only "many" are moved to believe in him?

A bit of reflection on the human condition helps us to understand the hesitancy to believe. All wanted to believe, because for each that would mean: God does love me and care for me; God is my friend; God will always be there when I need him. But they hesitated because they did not want others to think that they were rubes, not sophisticated, not "with it."

And a bit of reflection on my human condition makes this position even more understandable. I have seen miracles of grace in my life and in the lives of those around me. In response to these events, I've said, "That's it, never again a loss of faith," only to discover that forever can be a very short time.

Perhaps this is the lesson to be drawn from the resurrection of Lazarus. Faith is never, for any of us, a once-and-forever occurrence. Faith must be reaffirmed again and again.

Father, as I gather at the liturgy to be fed by your Word and the Eucharist of your Son, help me to affirm and reaffirm my faith in both these Words you have sent. May I make my own the prayer of St. Thomas the Apostle, "Lord, I do believe. Help my unbelief."

Conclusion

And so we come to the end of our in-depth reflection on the individual characters who have parts in the story of the passion and death of Jesus.

Hopefully these concentrated studies and the personal reflections which they prompt have helped us to attain the two aims which we had in mind when we set out on this journey through the story of the last hours of the life of Jesus. If we have moved even slightly towards the attainment of either of these goals, then these reflections have been truly profitable.

First, as we centered in on these individuals, we hoped to identify each one's strength or weakness of character. We then tried to make an application to our own lives of this strength or weakness.

Second, we hoped that looking closely, reflecting on the details of the story of each person involved in Jesus' passion, might help us to attain a fresher, deeper, and more effective appreciation of the story as a whole. Concentration on one part can help us to a fuller appreciation of the broad picture. The exercise is akin to trying to better appreciate a great painting by focusing in detail on one portion or one feature of the whole work.

The more we understand the suffering and death of Jesus, the closer we move toward appreciation of his life, toward love of his unbelievable sacrifice in dying for us and our sins, and toward eternal union with him in heaven.